# WRITE A NOVEL

# (In less than 60 days)

BY

Patrick Sullivan

Patrick Sullivan © 2020

## HOW TO START

Ok, so you have taken the first step to become a novelist. It does not take as much effort as you think to start the process. Everyone has something that they want to say but most people never put their thoughts on paper.

They often think it's too hard or they don't have the writing skills. This is not the truth, and this often stops people from writing and getting enjoyment out of it. Telling a story, reliving a past moment or giving the world a new adventure to become part of is what we all can bring to the table.

This book is going to give you some tips and tricks in getting started writing your first fictional novel. Use this book as a clipboard that allows you to be creative while following an outline. When you get started with your novel you may find that

Patrick Sullivan © 2020

this was just a springboard for you that showed you a way to get your message out to the world.

I am a novelist and my last novel followed these steps to the letter. It made it so much easier for me to complete the novel and get the story out. I wanted an easier process then I had used before. Here is what I came up with that worked very well for me.

To start with read this book through first and make notes as you go. Always keep a pen or pencil and paper handy. I know it is old school, but it works. When something pops into your mind jot it down that very moment. Don't wait or hold off until later, if you're like me you might lose that thought. Even if it is about another story/book idea. I have about 5 storylines going at any one time because of this. This allows you a great starting point to work from for future books.

Patrick Sullivan © 2020

Instead of an electronic version, you can always purchase this book in hardcopy format and make notes in it which is another great way of keeping your ideas and thoughts intact. Now let's get started so we can all see your novel in less than a few months.

Note:  Don't listen to everyone about how hard it is to write or get published. As I said read the book first then realize your dream of becoming a published novelist.

Starting a novel has a few but very important parts. Now here is the first trick and it's the all-important kick starter. Write about something you know something about or are very passionate about. It makes it so much easier to get the writing started and continued each day.

You will find that your mind will think about the book, it's plot, characters, twist and turns as well as alternate endings. Many famous authors stated that the plotline they started with was not how the book finished. When you are driving or trying to go to sleep at night all this will pop in your mind. Now don't go daydreaming, about the book, in a meeting. It's to soon to make this a new career but maybe one day. So, the term is "Passion with Control".

As that passion starts your mind racing think about what type of genre you are going to write about. Since we are talking about fictional novels in this book it would be in the fiction section of novel types. Writing about non-fiction such as this type of book is a different format and concept so I will not be covering it here.

Let's use the murder mystery genre for our example here. Don't worry about the title of your new book, it will hit you later. Sometimes, if you select one first, you focus on making the book about the title and it might change the direction you wanted it to go. You might also need to modify it or even change it all together when you do some research and find the title is already used. So, at the start of your new novel, it is not very important.

We have our genre and now on to our next step. Grab you a handful of 3x5 cards and think of your main characters. Let's say Brad is your hero and you need to capture him in your writing. Place his name at the top of one of the 3x5 cards and then below his name start placing his stats. Height, weight, the color of hair, build and education to start with. Write down as many things as you can think of to capture the picture of this character in your mind. It may take more than one 3x5 card for this character. Now do this for each main character in your novel. Capture everything you can think of and see in your mind. You then can write down the names of some of the minor characters and what they do on other cards. Don't go crazy with the character names. I know it is easy to also go to simple as well. Not everyone can be John Doe so remember that the names need to be easy to remember and unique at the same time. Don't make to many names close either. That will confuse the reader as the story progresses. Don't try and create a new language for your novel. That will also confuse and frustrate a reader.

Now tape or tac them up around your writing area. You will be able to quickly refer to them and keep from mixing up your characters as you write. This helps in keeping your writing going as well as fewer story edits because you mixed up a character's name halfway through your novel.

Patrick Sullivan © 2020

Ok, now back to Brad. He is blond, blue eyes, 6'2" and about 250 lbs. He works out a lot and has a strong build with tan skin. He works as a helpdesk technician in a large electronic firm or company. Now here is his information but it is best to put it on your 3x5 card in bullet format. You want to be able to refer to it at a glance, not have to read it each time. These cards will also help you when you think you are stuck. Don't worry if you start talking to these characters. You're not crazy, you're letting them speak to you as you press on with your story.

Brad Wonch

- Blond

- Blue eyes

- 6'2"

- 250 lbs

- IT Geek – Large corp

- And so on …

As you do this for each character you will have them come alive. You can see how they fit in a story or what they would or would not do. Add a little quirk to them that will give them character. Something like he has a habit of always having a toothpick in his mouth or she likes to draw in a mole on her left cheek. Something that will bring them to light in your story. Sometimes it is a way for the hero to find the killer. It does make your characters alive to the reader. If you can draw or sketch them do one of each character or find a picture of someone that looks like your character. Little tricks like that will keep the story flowing and give you a lot of ideas to write about.

Some tricks will help as well. I like to find props to place around me in my office to look at and get ideas or use to describe an object. One of my major issues when I first started writing was the description of things. My wife would always point out to me that a sword was not just a sword. She wanted me to describe it in my books with far more detail. Give the reader the chance to see what you are seeing when you write.  She pointed to two swords I had in my office. "Are they the same", she asked me? I, of course, would tell her no and then she would ask me to tell her why in detail. Once I started looking at them from a sharper point of view, I could see her point. One was curved with one side of the blade sharpen to slashing while the other was a sword used for strike attacks and sharpened on both sides of the blade. It had a red handle made up of strips of leather and so on. I'm sure you get the point as to how props could help to start with. The trick is to show the reader not tell them. This also works for the environment they are in and the background of each character. Show them what time of year or weather they are having don't tell the reader the information you will sound like a weatherman.

Now the last step of our prep work is to gather any research you will need. Most people forget this part before starting their novel and then halfway into their masterpiece they run into a snag. The streets don't line up or the timelines and dates do work. That's because they did not do a little research upfront.

You don't have to be writing a historical novel to need research. Research, to me, is as much fun as the novel itself. I started a novel recently about the missing treasure of the Knights Templar. So I read and researched everything I could get my hands on and now that I have completed my research I am finding that writing the novel is even going much faster then I expected.

Find out what time in history you want your novel to take place. You can't have a 1965 Ford Mustang in your character's driveway if the time is set in 1930. I know that is a big gap but look at how many times people point out movie mistakes with things like watches on characters in a William Wallace movie. Readers will focus on those types of mistakes and not enjoy the novel after that. Many times, they will put down your novel and never pick it back up. That throws future novels out the window for those readers. Don't forget about the reviews you will get as well.  If your character has diabetes, for example, then you need to make sure you understand what that means to him and what medicines he might need or what he should not eat. Things like that make a big difference in your novel and add a level of detail that readers look for.

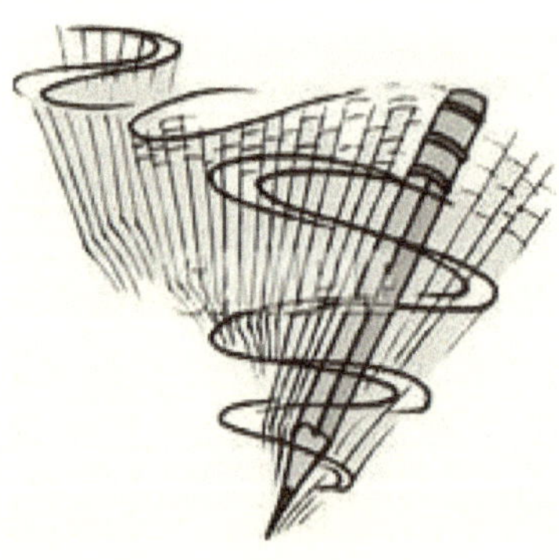

Notes:

# ENVIRONMENT

This next chapter is more about you setting up to write but just as important as any other aspect. The problem you will find is that not many "How to Write Books" talk about or emphasize the need for this important part of writing. Without the proper writing environment, you will never get anything written that has consistent flow as well as depth.

What do I mean about a writer's environment? The first thing is very obvious and that is a place to write. It needs to be a place that you will not be interrupted. That means a place that no one will bother you or odd sounds that will distract you for the time you have set aside to write.

Now, unless you have a soundproof room you're going to hear sounds and that's ok. They can add to the story, such as traffic, birds or wind blowing the leaves around. You can use those sounds to add to your story and create a real environment for your characters. It works very well to have that real feel incorporated into the book. However, sounds that are very loud or distracting that do not add to your story will hinder your writing and story progress.

Now I have known writers that have an office, a desk in a bedroom or on the balcony. I have even known writers that have purchased a shed from the local store and outfitted it with the things they need to begin their writing careers. Whatever you need to get yourself prepared to write only you can determine that, not any other writers. Each of use have a needed and often very different environment in which to write. I do love learning about the different places authors choose so let me know what you have chosen.

Patrick Sullivan © 2020

So, you're in the writing area that you feel is the best place to get your story started and the creative juices flowing. The next thing you need to do is place things around you that you can draw inspiration from. Remember I talked about the description of items being so very important. This is how I get the detail I need in my stories.

If I am writing about a warrior that has a knife or sword it helps me to have one to view and even sometimes hold to get the feel and look of the item to come alive on the page. Think about how much easier it is to describe something you have in your hands or right in front of you and not just from your mind.

A picture is worth a thousand words they say so reverse that and say a thousand words can describe a picture. I'm not going to sit here and bore you with a ton of examples, you can imagine all the things you could surround yourself with that would inspire your mind and enhance the story. Don't be afraid to change out the props or add to your writing area. I added shelves to bring in more items and sometimes I mix and match items to create new things in my books. Just as a word of warning if you borrow your spouse's stuff from her office take it back when you're done.

The last thing we need to do before we start is to select how much time and when you are going to write. It sounds easy but once you set a schedule do your best to stick to it. Inform everyone that this is your time and not to interrupt you unless it is very important.

Now here is a very important aspect of this part of the plan. Don't have an attitude about being left alone. Just help them understand how important it is to you and ask for their help. That will go a long way in getting cooperation and you will have peace of mind as you sit down to write. A good attitude on your part brings a better-written word out of you.

You're going to ask how long of a time will you need each writing day. This will vary with each writer. Your goal is six pages a day. So how long that takes you is the time you set aside for yourself. Your first novel will be a test case for you to see what that time is. The subsequent novels will be much easier as you have the experience from the first one to go by. Now let's get writing our first novel.

Patrick Sullivan © 2020

## OUTLINE

I will be using 10 chapters, 30 pages per chapter for this example so that you can see how easy it is to write a book in less than 60 days. So, to start with we have picked our genre, selected our main and minor characters with descriptions. We have gathered the research we needed for our novel. We have our writing area all set up, so we are ready to start writing correct? Well, almost just one more little thing to do before you sit down. Get yourself something to drink, a pad of paper & pen to jot down notes on, a snack if needed.

Now let's start creating an outline for our new novel. Don't worry about a table of contents until the end. In many novels, writers don't use them so we don't need to stress about that when we start. Think of each chapter as a scene in a movie or play. You have something that needs to happen here to develop your story. You need to know where the scene will take place and who will be in the scene. I love bullet points so start jotting down the outline of that first chapter.

- Where is this scene taking place?

- Who is in the scene?

- What is the scene about?

- What do you need to get out of the scene to have the chapter complete?

If you have ever watched a crime show you have seen the police use a murder room. This is almost what you will do to ensure your plot works. Don't limit yourself with too few bullet points. Keep adding detail to the bullet points so that you can understand what is taking place in the chapter when you come back to the outline to start writing. Don't worry about editing your outline, who cares if it is not grammatically correct its not your novel, it's just an outline.

Once you have completed chapter one then do the same thing for the next nine chapters until you are complete with all chapter outlines. This helps to ensure your story will be consistent and you don't leave out an important scene that ties it all together at the end.

Now if you are using a writing program make ten folders and save each chapter in their separate folder. This is important in keeping your writing flowing and not rereading your novel every few pages. Also, save your work often, there is nothing worse than losing an hour's worth of effort because you forgot to save and the power went out or the program crashed or something worse. I even go the old school route and print off each time I finish for the day and place the new pages in folders I have on my desk. That just helps me when I decided to edit the novel.

## BODY OF YOUR NOVEL

I hope you're excited by now and ready to get started so let's do that very thing. Start with your chapter one outline. Before you get started writing here are some rules you must use to give yourself every chance in the world to have this novel written in less than 60 days.

Do not, and I repeat, do not edit as you write. It is going to be one of the hardest things you will ever do but it is one of the most important. Let the words flow from your fingers and your mind. Don't stop the rhythm you get into by rereading your work ever few sentences or perform a spell check to see what you misspelled. Your auto correct option will catch a lot of your mistyping and other free grammar checking applications can help you later.

I have seen writers spend weeks on a chapter that should have taken them days. The problem was that they went back every day and reread the entire chapter making corrections. At that rate, they will never get the novel ready for print. Once you have finished your six pages for that day save the file and do not read it or any other pages of the book you have already written. If you have additional thoughts you want to add, jot down the information and keep it for later. I'll tell you when to introduce that information.

As you open your outline you will see the information you placed there and now you remember what you wanted to have happened in that chapter. You start but grabbing your reader's attention with some kind of action, shocking issue or thought-provoking moment. If you don't grab your reader in the first couple of pages they will never read your novel. You may have written the next top-selling novel but if you can't get them to read it, it will not matter.

Don't forget to look at each of your character cards and get to know them. You want your readers to understand them and grow to care about them or hate them depending on their roll. You also want to make sure you don't have them do something that would be out of character. That is a sure fired way of losing your reader and creating a book that is impossible to follow.

At the end of each 6-page day save your work and, as I have stated before, do not go back and reread any prior work you have created. Each page should have between 300 – 400 words on the page depending on the beginning or end of a chapter, the number of paragraphs on the page can change the word count. In approximately 5 writing days, you should have a chapter, un-edited of course, toward your novel.

When you have completed the chapter save it and put it away. You will not be looking at it for a little while. Don't peak at all until you have finished the last chapter. That is very important to this process.

Now bring out the next outline and let's get started with chapter two. The process will not change at all through each chapter, No peaking, editing or rereading of chapters.

This is also very important if you skip a day of writing or you did not get six full pages out that day don't try to make up for it the next writing day. That will make the writing become a chore and not a fun activity. Writing a novel should be fun and not something you do not look forward to. If it becomes that take some time off and do some research for your next novel or go entertain yourself in another way.

Now we have 50 writing days behind us and we just finished chapter ten. Save it, of course, get up and walk away. You have a 300+ page novel rough draft completed in 50 days.

Patrick Sullivan © 2020

Great job but we are not finished just yet. Give yourself a week off at the very least.


Notes:

## EDITING BEGINS

Now the fun begins as you have taken off a week or so. You want to get the novel out of your head for a very important reason. What you have just written on paper maybe a little different then what you had in your mind. So let's see what you have written.

Pull out chapter one and take the notes, if any, you have written to incorporate into the chapter. You might have written a twist into the chapter that you thought of later in your writing. If it helps with the story or adds to a scene then great plug all of them into place. After you have placed the additions, start with page one and read your masterpiece. Don't worry you're going to get to a part where you go "what was I try to say here". We all do and it will happen in every chapter. Make the corrections to the section in question so that the reader will understand what you are trying to say. Make all your editing corrections for the entire chapter, save and then put it away for the second time. The same rules apply here, no going back once you have read and edited the chapter.

Do the same for all ten chapters and then walk away for a day or two. I know it sounds strange but you want to clear your mind from reading words, punctuation or descriptions into your novel that are not there. You will laugh when you find them and wonder how did I read that earlier when it was not there. As a special note here, if you find that you forgot to add something in an earlier chapter use the same rule you did when you first started. You take the information down and keep it for this last editing session.

Now that you have a day or so to rest your ready for the final stage. Go back and add any notes you have left for yourself. Once that is completed read the first chapter making final corrections. Do this for all chapters and save each chapter as you complete them. WOW, you have just completed your first novel

and are ready for the next step.


Notes:

## CONFIGURING YOUR BOOK LAYOUT

If you are thinking of artwork for your book you can add them one of two ways to start with. You can use art that is free and fits the image you have in mind or you can have it drawn for you. Either way, this might take some time so make sure, if you have someone going to do your artwork that they get started on that as soon as you have your outline completed. The only danger in that is if your plot changes in the middle of your writing your graphics might change as well.

If you self-publish the page outline is in the application they have you use and it makes it very easy to modify your document by just resizing your novel. They will ask you for your title and description to start with. Most of the self-publishing applications also have a cover generator built-in so that you can build your cover right there and not have to design one on your own. If you have one already then just upload it in the application. You can be on your way to having your novel published in a matter of hours.

I used Kindle Direct Publishing for this book as an example of how easy it was to setup. It took me about a half-hour to type in my bio, create a cover select fonts and play around with different cover art. Take some time to play around with the cover art if you don't have one that you already created. Don't just go to the section you are writing about look through all the artwork and pictures.

If you are trying to have your novel published by a publishing company then they will handle all that for you. Now it is time to enjoy your accomplishment.

Patrick Sullivan © 2020

There are further things you can do such as advertising and getting the word out about your new novel but that's for another book. Thank you for reading this book and please start your novel now and enjoy it. Good Luck!

Patrick Sullivan © 2020

Notes:

# ACKNOWLEDGMENTS

This book is dedicated to:

My Wife, for all her long hours of editing my Novels.